Pushing

A Modern Pranic Parable

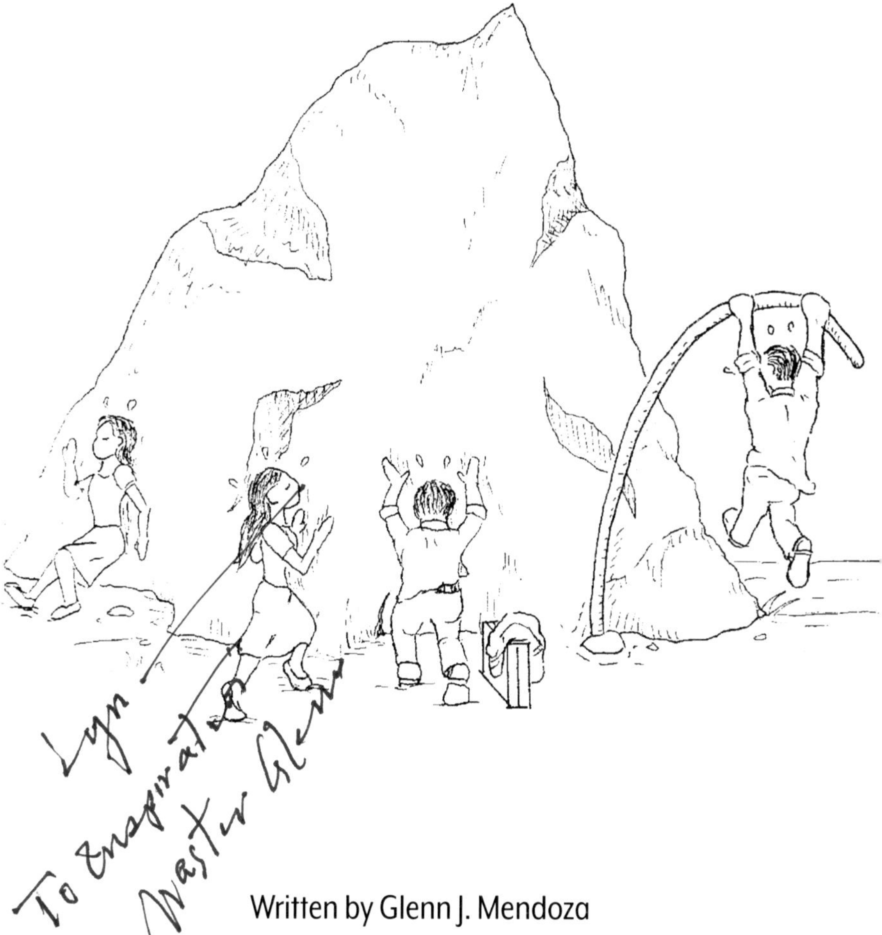

Lyn
To Inspiration
Master Glenn

Written by Glenn J. Mendoza
Illustrated by Stephen C. Lott

Pushing the Boulder
A Modern Pranic Parable

Copyright @ 2019 by Unicorn Light Publishing Company.
All rights reserved.

No part of this book may be reproduced in any form or by any means,
electronic or mechanical, including photocopying, recording, or by any
information storage and retrieval system, without permission in writing
from the publisher.

ISBN 978-0-9859708-2-6

Request for permission to reproduce selections
from this book should be mailed to:
Unicorn Light Publishing Company
420 Valley Brook Avenue
Lyndhurst, New Jersey 07071

Published by Unicorn Light Publishing Company

Image of GrandMaster Choa Kok Sui courtesy of Hector S. Ramos.

GrandMaster Choa Kok Sui
Founder of Modern Pranic Healing and Arhatic Yoga

Dedicated to

All Pranic Healing Teachers who have been working hard to spread the work as they embody the fortitude, perspicacity, and wisdom of our Teacher, GrandMaster Choa Kok Sui.

Acknowledgments

We express our heartful indebtedness and deep sense of gratitude to Kris Mendoza of Maestro Filmworks, Marianne Chung, Sueli Parpinelli, Matt McClendon and Dawn Myers.

Pranic Healing is the world's fastest-growing complementary energy healing system. This no-touch energy healing modality is based on the fundamental principle that the body has an innate ability to heal itself. By applying "life force" or prana, this healing process is accelerated. It is practiced by hundreds of thousands across the world to enhance all aspects of life.

Arhatic Yoga is a comprehensive system of spiritual practices that can accelerate one's spiritual evolution. GrandMaster Choa Kok Sui organized the system of Arhatic Yoga to balance Universal Love, Intelligence and Will. People from many different religions and philosophical traditions throughout the world practice this powerful system of spiritual growth.

The Spiritual Teacher plays a crucial role in the spiritual aspirant's journey. The Spiritual Teacher influences the disciple's root thinking and turns it to a bounteous understanding of life, a plenteous knowledge of the soul, and a deeper understanding of and reverence for God. The spiritual teacher leaves an indelible mark on the disciple's soul.

> *"The vital work of moving Pranic Healing and Arhatic Yoga forward does not wait to be done by perfect and enlightened men and women. It depends on a loving heart, a desire to serve, and unwavering faith in the True Spiritual Teacher."*
>
> — Glenn J. Mendoza

We were in darkness.
"We were sleeping."

Our lives seemed to have little purpose or meaning.

When Master Choa Kok Sui and
Pranic Healing appeared, we were inspired.

Our Souls were blessed and our
Higher Souls rejoiced.

Master told us to spread his and the Great Teacher's work.

He symbolically showed us a large boulder,
representing the challenges we will have to face.

Master Choa explained that we have to
push against the boulder with all our might if
we were to spread his work.

So we did...

day after day, week after week,
month after month, year after year.

For years, even after Master left us physically,

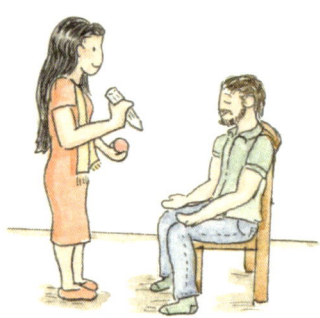

we worked from sun up to sun down, spreading the work.

We kept pushing the immovable boulder with all our might.

Each weekend, we returned from traveling and teaching;

bodies weary and at times wondering if our efforts had been in vain.

Our lower nature placed thoughts into
our tired and doubting minds:

"You have been spreading
the teachings and pushing
against that boulder for
years, and it has
not moved."

Our lower nature gave us the impression that the
task was impossible and that we were a failure.
These thoughts discouraged and disheartened us.

Our lower self said, "Why
are you working so hard?
Just put in your time,
give the minimum effort;
that will be good enough."

It was tempting at times, but we took our troubled thoughts to Master in our meditation.

"Master, Master," we implored our Teacher, "We have worked long and hard in your service, putting all our energy into doing what you've asked. Yet, after all this time, we've not moved the boulder. We cannot seem to spread the work the way you want. What is wrong? Why are we failing?"

Then Master responded compassionately,
"**My dear chelas, when I asked you to serve me and you accepted, I told you that your task was to spread the teachings and push against the boulder with all your strength, which you have done.**"

"**Never once did I mention that I expected you to move it. Your work was to push. Now you come to me with your energy spent, blaming yourself that you have failed. But, is that really so?**"

"Look at yourself. Your Physical Body is healthy and strong. Your Emotional Body is stable. Your Mind and Mental Body are sharp and have experienced dramatic shifts."

"Your Energy Body and chakras have grown tremendously, and your connection to your Higher Soul is strong. Through trials, you have grown and your skills and abilities now surpass that which you used to have."

"It is true, you have not moved the boulder. But your calling was to follow simple instructions; to push and exercise your faith in me and My Teacher's wisdom."

"Now my chelas, I will move the boulder."

At times, we become distressed asking,
"What does Master want us to do?
What are we suppose to accomplish?"

What Master really wants from us is trust,
humility and unwavering faith in him.
"Things will happen," he said,
"you do not have to do everything."

By all means, let us exercise the faith that
moves mountains, maintain our practice,
and spread the teachings; but always know
that it is Master, his Great Teacher and
company who are moving the Work.

When

pranic healing work & arhatic yoga

gets you down.

When everything seems to go wrong...

and be out of control...

just relax
be patient
have faith

When you argue with other chelas,
other teachers, other students...

and your patience is getting thin, and
your temper is getting shorter...

Just direct your attention to...

and things will be resolved.

When you feel misunderstood and alone...

Just trust in
Master Choa Kok Sui and
in his Great Teacher,
Mahaguruji Mei Ling.

atma namaste!

May the Blessings of God,
Master Choa Kok Sui and
Lord Mahaguruji Mei Ling be
upon you, your family and
your Pranic Healing group.